Girls Hold Up This World

By **JADA PINKETT SMITH**

Photographs by **DONYELL KENNEDY-McCULLOUGH**

Cartwheel BOOKS®

Scholastic Inc.   New York Toronto London Auckland Sydney Mexico City New Delhi Hong Kong Buenos Aires

Library of Congress Cataloging-in-Publication Data

Pinkett, Jada.
Girls hold up this world / by Jada Pinkett Smith.
 p. cm.
Summary: Relates how girls are unique individuals,
possessing self-esteem and discipline, and able to work with
other girls to make the world a better place.

ISBN 0-439-08793-7 -- ISBN 0-439-11332-6 (pbk.)

[1. Girls--Fiction. 2. Conduct of life--Fiction.]   I. Title. II.
PZ7.P6332 Gi 2003   [E]--dc21   2002014560

12 11 10 9 8 7 6 5 4 3 2 1   05 06 07 08 09

Printed in Mexico   49
First printing, February 2005
Book design by Elizabeth B. Parisi

For my Meme, Bernice V. Kennedy,
thank you for my past.
For my Mommy, Therese White,
thank you for the present.
And my daughter, Kennedy-Rue, thank
you, thank you, thank you for the future!
— D. K-M

I would like to thank all the girls and
women who made this book possible, you
know who you are. Thank you, Mommie.
— J.P.S

For Marion Martin Banfield
January 9, 1915 — Eternity

— J.P.S.

We girls hold up this world   with a

strength that's all our own.

We'll see
the different ways
one day when
we are grown.

When we show our softer side, that doesn't mean we're weak.

We're made up of many emotions

that make us
each unique.

B e proud

o be a girl — know what it means to you.

Be who you
want to be — don't doubt
the things you do.

W e girls
hold up this world
as we build
our self-esteem.

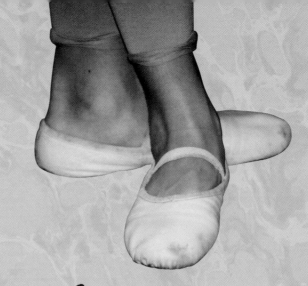

We know that
discipline will turn a princess
into a queen.

Kindness takes hard work — this is a lifelong lesson.

Give from your heart,
and each day
will be a blessing.

We are sisters of this Earth — members of one powerful tribe.

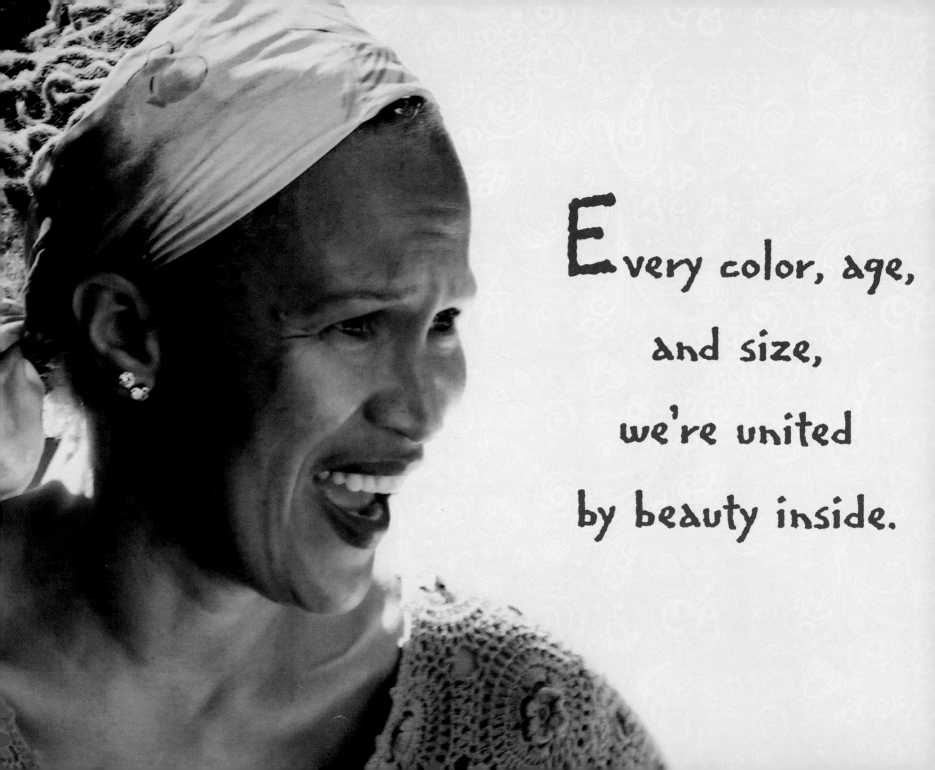

Every color, age,
and size,
we're united
by beauty inside.

We're a new generation of girls — we will make this world better.

We girls hold up this world,

standing united....

Standing together!